D1717047

21st Century Disasters

Indian Ocean Earthquake and Tsunami

by Stephanie Bearce

FOCUS READERS

BEACON

www.focusreaders.com

Focus Readers is distributed by North Star Editions:
sales@northstareditions.com | 888-417-0195

Produced for Focus Readers by Red Line Editorial.

Photographs ©: Suzanne Plunkett/AP Images, cover, 1; Food Travel Stockforlife/Shutterstock Images, 4; AFP/Getty Images, 7; Red Line Editorial, 9; Gemunu Amarasinghe/AP Images, 10; Stefano Ember/ Shutterstock Images, 13; Yarr65/Shutterstock Images, 14; Denis Costille/Shutterstock Images, 16–17, 29; Frans Delian/Shutterstock Images, 18, 21, 24; Photography by Mangiwau/Moment/Getty Images, 23; BNK Maritime Photographer/Shutterstock Images, 27

Library of Congress Cataloging-in-Publication Data
Names: Bearce, Stephanie, author.
Title: Indian Ocean earthquake and tsunami / by Stephanie Bearce.
Description: Lake Elmo, MN : Focus Readers, 2020. | Series: 21st century
   disasters | Includes index. | Audience: Grade 4 to 6.
Identifiers: LCCN 2019002271 (print) | LCCN 2019010423 (ebook) | ISBN
   9781641859486 (PDF) | ISBN 9781641858793 (ebook) | ISBN 9781641857413
   (hardcover) | ISBN 9781641858106 (pbk.)
Subjects: LCSH: Indian Ocean Tsunami, 2004--Juvenile literature. |
   Tsunamis--Indian Ocean--Juvenile literature. | Earthquakes--Indian
   Ocean--Juvenile literature.
Classification: LCC GC221.5 (ebook) | LCC GC221.5 .B45 2020 (print) | DDC
   909/.098240831--dc23
LC record available at https://lccn.loc.gov/2019002271

Printed in the United States of America
Mankato, MN
May, 2019

About the Author

Stephanie Bearce is a history detective who loves doing experiments and working in her makerspace. One of her favorite things to make is books! She has written more than 20 books for kids and is always writing and researching new stories.

Table of Contents

Chapter 1

A Wall of Water

December 26, 2004, began as a beautiful day in Thailand. Ten-year-old Tilly Smith was at the beach with her family. The sun sparkled on the blue water.

Thailand is known for its many beautiful beaches.

Tilly watched people swim and wade. Then she noticed something strange. The water rushed away from the shore.

Tilly remembered a lesson from science class. When water rushes away, it's a sign that a **tsunami** is coming. Tilly knew that she had to warn people.

Did You Know?

The tsunami's waves were more than 100 feet (30 m) tall.

 Tsunami waves rush toward a beach in Thailand.

Tilly and her family ran back to their hotel for help. Hotel workers hurried people off the beach. A few seconds later, a wall of water hit the shore. Tilly's quick thinking saved hundreds of lives. But other people were not as lucky.

The tsunami killed more than 225,000 people that day. It was one of the deadliest natural disasters in history.

The tsunami was caused by an **earthquake** in the Indian Ocean. This earthquake sent huge waves toward the coast. When the waves

Did You Know?

The earthquake that caused the 2004 tsunami was the second-largest earthquake ever measured.

TSUNAMI TIMELINE

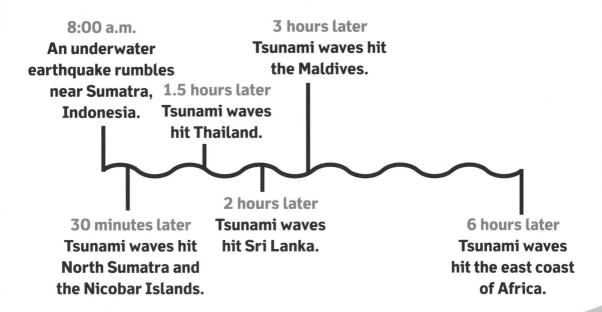

8:00 a.m.
An underwater earthquake rumbles near Sumatra, Indonesia.

1.5 hours later
Tsunami waves hit Thailand.

3 hours later
Tsunami waves hit the Maldives.

30 minutes later
Tsunami waves hit North Sumatra and the Nicobar Islands.

2 hours later
Tsunami waves hit Sri Lanka.

6 hours later
Tsunami waves hit the east coast of Africa.

arrived, they ripped up roads and buildings.

The tsunami hit Indonesia the hardest. But it affected 13 other countries, too. Many were left with huge areas of flooding and damage.

Chapter 2

Understanding Tsunamis

Some tsunamis are caused by volcanoes or landslides. However, most tsunamis happen because of underwater earthquakes. These earthquakes begin deep beneath the floor of the ocean.

 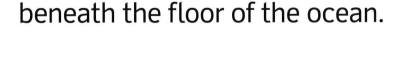

Waves from the 2004 tsunami rush past houses in Sri Lanka.

They are caused by the movement of Earth's **crust**. Earth's crust is made up of huge pieces called plates. The plates float on **molten** rock. They move very slowly.

Sometimes, plates crash or rub together. When this happens, the plates release energy. The energy

Did You Know?

A tsunami wave can reach speeds of 500 miles per hour (805 km/h). It can cross an ocean in just a few hours.

 A tsunami's waves fill streets with debris.

causes the ocean floor to tremble and shake. The water moves, too. A wave forms at the water's surface. The wave may begin far out at sea. But it travels toward the coast.

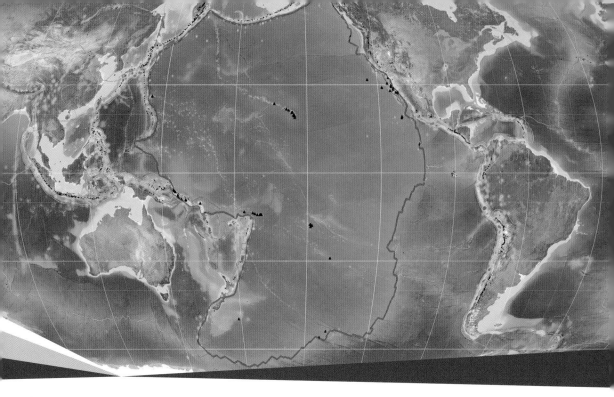

The red line in this image shows the Ring of Fire, which runs around the Pacific Ocean.

As the wave moves, it gathers energy and speed. It grows tall as it nears the shore. It hits the land as a huge wall of water.

The rushing water is dangerous. It can crush houses and cars. It can toss huge boats. Most tsunamis hit as a series of waves. The danger is not over until after the last wave has hit.

Many tsunamis happen in the Ring of Fire. This area is located in the Pacific Ocean. The area contains more than 400 volcanoes. Earthquakes are common there, too.

Did You Know?

Approximately 80 percent of tsunamis happen in the Ring of Fire.

Tsunamis

Before a tsunami hits, the water will often pull back from the shore. It looks like **low tide**. But this means a huge wave is coming. People may hear a loud roar. Or the ground may shake.

People near coasts should watch for these signs. If any appear, people must go to higher ground right away. There may be only minutes until the first wave hits.

A person caught in a tsunami should grab something that floats. It is safer to float than swim. Dangerous **debris** under the water can hurt people.

A sign warns beach visitors to watch for tsunamis.

Chapter 3

Survivor Stories

The 2004 tsunami left more than 1.7 million people homeless. One was 17-year-old Marthunis. On the day of the tsunami, he was playing soccer with friends. They felt the earthquake and ran home.

 Many camps took in people who lost their homes in the tsunami.

Marthunis's family tried driving to safety. However, the roads were full. When the tsunami hit, water swept over the family's van. Marthunis saw a wooden chair float by. He grabbed the chair and drifted in the water. He didn't let go until he came to a beach.

Marthunis was alone for 20 days. Finally, rescue workers found him. They took him to a hospital, where he saw his father. Sadly, the rest of his family had not survived.

 Many people lost their houses and everything they owned.

The tsunami caused many deaths. Nearly 150,000 children became **orphans**. One of them was 12-year-old Victor Israelsson.

21

He was on the beach with his family.

Suddenly, they saw a huge wave.

They started to run. Victor heard

a noise that sounded like a train.

Then a huge wave hit him.

Victor felt like he was inside

a washing machine. Bricks, tree

Did You Know?

Animals might hear sounds before
tsunamis, too. Before the waves
hit Sri Lanka, elephants ran from a
beach. Scientists think a low sound
warned them.

 Tsunami waves damaged much of Sri Lanka's coastline.

branches, and boards swirled around him. He fought to breathe. Finally, the wave threw him onto the shore. Victor was safe. But no one else in his family survived.

Chapter 4

Aftermath

It took years to repair the tsunami's damage. Workers had to fix roads and water supplies. Then, they rebuilt many houses, hospitals, and schools. Repairs cost several billion dollars.

The tsunami's strong waves smashed thousands of buildings.

Scientists didn't want such destruction to happen again. They needed a way to warn people. In 2005, the **United Nations** agreed to build a tsunami warning system. This system measures earthquakes in the Indian Ocean. Computers predict which countries a tsunami

Did You Know?

On average, two tsunamis hit somewhere in the world each year. An especially large tsunami tends to happen every 15 years.

 This tsunami detection buoy tracks changes in the ocean after an earthquake.

will hit. They can even guess when the waves will arrive. The system sends messages to people in those countries. The warning gives them more time to reach safety.

FOCUS ON

Indian Ocean Earthquake and Tsunami

Write your answers on a separate piece of paper.

1. Write a paragraph describing the warning signs of a tsunami.

2. Why do you think people visit beaches where tsunamis might happen?

3. What causes most tsunamis?
    - **A.** earthquakes
    - **B.** landslides
    - **C.** volcanoes

4. Why should people go to higher ground before a tsunami hits?
    - **A.** Higher ground is easier for boats to reach.
    - **B.** Higher ground does not have earthquakes.
    - **C.** Higher ground will not be covered by the tsunami's waves.

5. What does **affected** mean in this book?

The tsunami hit Indonesia the hardest. But it ***affected*** *13 other countries, too.*

> **A.** helped something improve
> **B.** made something smaller
> **C.** caused something to change

6. What does **predict** mean in this book?

Computers ***predict*** *which countries a tsunami will hit. They can even guess when the waves will arrive.*

> **A.** to study what has happened in the past
> **B.** to tell what will happen in the future
> **C.** to change what is happening now

Answer key on page 32.

Glossary

crust
Earth's hard outer layer.

debris
The remains of something broken.

earthquake
A sudden shaking of the ground that often causes damage and destruction.

low tide
The time when the water level along the coast is lowest. At low tide, water moves farthest back from the shore.

molten
Melted by intense heat.

orphans
Children whose parents have died.

tsunami
A huge wave of water, often one that causes massive damage when it hits the shore.

United Nations
A group of countries around the world that work together to solve problems.

To Learn More

BOOKS

Bailer, Darice. *Indian Ocean Tsunami Survival Stories*. Mankato, MN: The Child's World, 2016.

Squire, Ann O. *Tsunamis*. New York: Children's Press, 2016.

Ventura, Marne. *Detecting Tsunamis*. Lake Elmo, MN: Focus Readers, 2017.

NOTE TO EDUCATORS

Visit **www.focusreaders.com** to find lesson plans, activities, links, and other resources related to this title.

Index

C
crust, 12

E
earthquake, 8–9, 11, 15, 19, 26

I
Indian Ocean, 8, 26
Indonesia, 9

N
natural disaster, 8

P
Pacific Ocean, 15
plates, 12

R
Ring of Fire, 15

S
shore, 6–7, 14, 16, 23
Sri Lanka, 9, 22

T
Thailand, 5, 9

U
United Nations, 26

V
volcanoes, 11, 15

W
wave, 6, 8–9, 12–15, 16, 22–23, 27

Answer Key: 1. Answers will vary; **2.** Answers will vary; **3.** A; **4.** C; **5.** C; **6.** B